THE ONLY
CHARACTER
WORKBOOK
YOU'LL EVER NEED

Compiled by

_____

For project(s)

Series Bibles for
Writers

T.M. HOLLADAY

First published by Naniloa Books, 2020

Copyright © 2020 Series Bibles for Writers

Authored by T.M. Holladay

First edition.

My fellow writers,

If you're struggling to figure out what makes your villain tick, or if your characters all have the same voice, or if you've got a hot-mess of a character bible binder on your shelf filled with ideas scribbled on junk mail and old receipts, this workbook is going to be your new best friend.

Yes, these pages will organize your cast. But it will also help you understand them. Because the more you know about everything that makes a character unique, the more genuine they will feel to your readers. Their histories will shape them. Their personalities will ring true. Their vulnerabilities and emotional shields will explain their choices. And your writing will flow, baby. *Flow.*

The C H A R A C T E R P R O F I L E S contained herein are expansive. Obviously, you may not need to fill in every blank or answer every question, and you're probably not going to mention all the things in your novels, but the more you know, the more genuine your characters will read on the page. Because you will know them. Character voice? Check. Understandable logic? Double check. Immersing the reader into the story through characters they can feel? Super triple check.

The G R O U P L I S T S are for keeping track of the people and things in various groups, and the purpose and history of those groups. Who's on the king's council? Who's in the book club? Who lives in the village? What positions are in the military? Who are all of the suspects in the ship captain's murder? And while we're at it, what exactly were all of Voldemort's horcruxes? It takes me like twelve minutes to remember all of those accurately.

R E L A T I O N S H I P M A P S A N D F A M I L Y T R E E S might not be something you have done before. But you Because mapping out those interconnected relationships can lead to hella-awesome revelations. Weave the relationships and goals of secondary characters into conflict with the relationships and goals of your protagonist. Make choices harder for your characters because of the complicated connected-ness of other people in the story. Those map lines should cross and connect and triangulate into delicious, legendary tension. Dang, I can feel it already. This area is also a great place to sketch out any family trees, genealogy, or royal lines!

The N O T E S section is just that. It's where you unleash the info-dump of brainstorms, diagrams, sketches and all of the other things that get those creative juices flowing.

And at the back, you'll find a C H R O N O L O G I C A L L I S T list if you'd like to keep track of your characters as they appear in the story, and an A L P H A B E T I C A L L I S T list to keep track of every name.

So go for it. Lay it all out. Dig deep into the psyches. And this workbook will be here to keep the incredible, dreamy, gritty, intriguing, shocking, magical windstorms of creativity organized.

Here's to your next fantastic novel,

TM Holladay

PERSONALITIES   6

PRIMARY PROFILES   9

SECONDARY PROFILES   59

MINOR CHARACTERS   109

"The key to creating better plots rests in a deeper understanding of character."

— Kristen Lamb, *Great Characters - The Beating Heart of Great Fiction*

There are an abundance of personality tests out there. And by abundance, I mean literal thousands. For this workbook, you can use whichever one(s) you identify with the most. There are blank spaces for you to write in each primary and secondary character's personality results. If you are not attached to any particular personality assessment at the moment, might I offer a few suggestions?

The most prominent personality assessment is the MYERS-BRIGGS TYPE INDICATOR (MBTI), which uses four basic foundations (extrovert vs. introvert, feeling vs. thinking, sensing vs. intuition, and judging vs. perceiving) to outline sixteen in-depth and eye-opening personality types. The results are fascinating. And bonus, once you get the hang of it, assessing multiple characters can happen very quickly. I highly recommend the MBTI as a tool to help you flesh out your diverse cast. And because of its prominence, the wealth of information related to the MBTI is astounding. You can find blogs and sites and infographic resources that explain everything from what situations would anger each type, to how they deal with confrontation, to the type of person each type is naturally drawn to, to the spiritual gifts of different types. You can read more about the Myers-Briggs Type Indicator on their website, **myersbriggs.org.**

Another personality indicator I recommend (and have included directly on the character profiles) are the 5 LOVE LANGUAGES, by Dr. Gary Chapman. This assessment explains how an individual shows love or appreciation to others, and how that person prefers to receive love or appreciation. Outlining this one aspect of a character's personality might just be your top tool as a writer in discovering tension and resolution in your story. You can read more about those love languages and take the quiz at **5lovelanguages.com.**

And last but certainly not least, my favorite guide for creating relatable and genuine characters came via **Brené Brown's** book "**Daring Greatly**." There, she discusses seven different ways that people shield their vulnerabilities from other people. Author Melanie Jacobson had the brilliant idea of taking those VULNERABILITY SHIELDS and applying them to fiction characters. Because, though your character's vulnerabilities might explain their fears, hopes, and wants, their shields are what explain their reactions. If you want your character's choices to ring true, I highly recommend reading "Daring Greatly," focusing especially on chapter four, "The Vulnerability Armory" to get an in-depth understanding of those seven shields.

Brief infographic outlines of the Myers-Briggs Type Indicator, the Five Love Languages, and Brené Brown's vulnerability shields are provided on the following pages as a reference and are not intended to educate you on these concepts. Rather, (if you decide to include these indicators in your character profiling), the following outlines are meant to be used as a quick reminder after you have done the research needed to fully understand them.

And of course, if none of these float your boat, that's okay. Prefer using the Enneagram test? Why not? True Colors test? Go for it. Emotional Intelligence test? Love it. This workbook is meant to work for you, however you decide to go about it.

> "Personality plays a large role in how a character sounds. Their voice will reflect that personality and color every line of dialog and internal thought."

— Janice Hardy, *How To Write Characters Who Don't Sound Like You*

INTJ — The Mastermind / Architect

Comfortable alone. Self-sufficient. Needs to recharge after socializing. Interested in ideas and theories. Innovative. Questions why things happen the way they do. Excels at developing strategies. Doesn't like uncertainty.

INFJ — The Counselor / Advocate

Visionary, idealistic, insightful, dependable, gentle, creative. They have a different, profound way of looking at the world. Substance and depth, never accepting things the way they are. Perceived as weird or amusing. Seeks harmony, cooperation.

INTP — The Thinker / Logician

Most logical minded and precise of all. Loves patterns, keen eye for discrepancies, and a good ability to read people. Can catch liars easily. Not interested in day-to-day activities. Spends their time and energy on creative genius pursuits to reach their unbiased, problem solving potential.

INFP — The Idealist / Mediator

Quiet, reserved, sensitive, perceptive, loyal, caring, poetic, dreamy, altruistic, poetic. Prefers not to talk about themselves. Prefers time alone in quiet places where they can make sense of what is happening around them. Analyzes symbols as metaphors. Often lost in dreams and possibilities. Values inner harmony and growth.

ENTJ — The Commander

Uses a rational, logical approach on external aspects. Uses intuition and reasoning on internal aspects. Natural born leader. Strategic, efficient, ambitious. Long-range planner. Lives in a world of possibilities. Sees challenges as opportunities to push themselves. Makes decisions quickly yet carefully. Does not like to sit still.

ENFJ — The Giver / Protagonist

People-focused. Skilled communicator. Idealistic, charismatic, outspoken, diplomatic, highly principled and ethical. Understands how to connect with all types, values connection. Relies on intuition and feelings. Tends to live in the abstract or their imagination rather than in the real world. Thinks of possible futures.

ENTP — The Visionary / Defender

Rare. Extroverted, but does not enjoy small talk. Intelligent and knowledgeable, needs to be constantly mentally stimulated. Discusses theories and facts in extensive detail. Logical, rational, and objective in their approach to information and arguments. Inventive, strategic, versatile, enterprising, inquisitive. Values inspiration.

ENFP — The Champion / Campaigner

Individualistic. Creators of their own methods, looks, actions, and ideas. Does not like cookie cutter people and hates when forced inside a box. Strong intuition, operates from their feelings. Highly perceptive and thoughtful. Social, supportive, playful, and sees potential in others. Enjoys new projects.

ISTJ — The Inspector

Serious, quiet, thorough, responsible, sincere, analytical, dependable, systematic, trustworthy, hardworking, with sound, practical judgement. Interested in security and peaceful living. Well-developed powers of concentration. Promotes tradition and cultural responsibility.

ISTP — The Craftsman / Virtuoso

Mysterious, rational, analytical. Also quite spontaneous, enthusiastic, and unpredictable, though they hide those traits from the outside world, often very successfully. They enjoy adventure, and are action-oriented, independent, reserved. Understands tools and the mechanics of things.

ISFJ — The Nurturer / Defender

Philanthropist. Returns generosity with even more generosity. Devoted, unselfish caretaker and friend. Warm, kind-hearted. Values harmony and cooperation, and likely sensitive to other people's feelings. People value them for their consideration and awareness, and their ability to bring out the best in others.

ISFP — The Composer / Adventurer

Introvert that sees value in meeting new people. Difficulty connecting at first, but eventually becomes warm, approachable, and friendly. Fun, spontaneous. Tags along in whatever activity. Lives life to the fullest, embraces the present. Always exploring and discovering. They find wisdom in experiences.

ESTJ — The Supervisor / Executive

Organized, honest, dedicated, dignified, traditional, and a great believer of doing what they believe is right and correct. A Leader, even on hard paths. Epitome of good citizenry. Happy when approached for help. People look to them for guidance and counsel.

ESTP — The Doer / Entrepreneur

Outgoing, realistic, curious, versatile. Governed by a need for social interaction. Emotional, logical. Has a need for freedom. Uninterested in theories and abstracts. Leaps before they look, fixing their mistakes as they go. Pragmatic problem solver and skillful negotiator.

ESFJ — The Provider / Consul

Social butterfly. Their need to interact with others and make people happy usually ends up making them popular. Friendly, reliable, conscientious, outgoing. Seeks to be helpful. Revels in the spotlight and organizing social events. Enjoys being active and productive.

ESFP — The Performer / Entertainer

Observant, enthusiastic, fun, friendly, tactful, flexible. Feels and perceives personalities. Strong common sense. Enjoys spotlight. Loves learning and sharing what they learn with others. Strong interpersonal skills. Warm, generous, sympathetic, and concerned for other people's well-being.

Visit myersbriggs.org to read the full profiles for each of these types and to take and understand the assessment.

Most people have a primary love language, but still identify with other languages as well, in a ranked order.

Physical Touch

Feeling or expressing love through physical touch & accessibility, including kissing, cuddling, holding hands, and sex.

Acts of Service

Showing love by completing tasks and/or actions to ease the burdens or responsibilities of others.

Words of Affirmation

Expressing sincere verbal or written compliments or other words of praise and appreciation.

Quality Time

Spending time together, being present, giving full undivided attention to show love and consideration.

Receiving Gifts

Receiving or giving thoughtful gifts and gestures as a symbol of love or appreciation.

Visit 5lovelanguages.com to take and understand the assessment, and to learn more about each language.

VULNERABILITY SHIELDS

Most people have more than one shield. The vast majority of people do identify with at least one of these top three shields.

Foreboding Joy/Rehearsing Tragedy

Always looking behind the door of anything good that happens so they aren't caught off guard. They expect bad things in order to avoid disappointment. (Like a mother constantly thinking if her new baby is going to get sick, or a man constantly expecting his wife to leave him.)

Perfectionism

Pretending and performing perfection in order to avoid shame and judgment. This is not actually self-improvement. They seek approval from others. By presenting a "perfected" image, they believe they are hiding their insecurities or fears from the world around them.

Numbing

Embracing whatever deadens the pain and discomfort of shame. Examples include alcohol, drugs, and sex, but other common and more subtle things include busyness, over-eating, over-working, and over-buying.

These last four shields are usually present alongside one of the top three shields.

Victim-Viking

They are scared to be a victim, so they choose to dominate or elevate themselves above others instead. Their natural inclination is to be above in order to avoid being a victim. They fear victimization.

Let It All Hang Out

Floodlighting: oversharing as a defense against true vulnerability to immediately see if another person can handle it. They are looking for who they can trust with their "issues" and who they can't trust.

Serpentining

Backing out, pretending not to care, or pretending that it is not happening at all. Hiding out, avoidance, procrastination, rationalizing, blaming, and lying, all of which usually involves more energy than facing the problem. Energy spent avoiding is greater than dealing with their painful vulnerabilities.

Cynicism-Criticism-Cool-Cruelty

Used as a weapon. They move attention away from vulnerabilities and toward "coolness." Examples include smart-aleck commentary, gossiping, snarkiness, dark humor, and making fun of others. They think enthusiasm and engagement are signs of gullibility. They try to distract and deceive those around them.

Visit brenebrown.com/books-audio to find the book or audio of "Daring Greatly" available at your preferred retailer.

PRIMARY CHARACTERS

"When you force the character to do something in the story that is in direct conflict with a core value, or have two core values (or two sides of the same core value) clash, you ramp up your story's suspense and give your writing an underlying, subtle, but strong tension beneath the surface."

— Kathy Steffen, *Core Character Values: Finding the Moral Compass*

OTHER NAMES
(titles, ranks,
pseudonyms)

Age (at intro.)

Gender

Group,
classification,
or species

MC/Protag	Deuteragonist	Antagonist	Secondary	Foil/Contrast	Love Interest	Mentor	Narrator	Confidant	

Birthdate

Birth place

Parents

Education

Ancestry

Social class

Religion

Sexuality

Significant past

Residence

Living with

Occupation

Income

Death?

(attach or sketch image here)

PHYSICAL DESCRIPTION

Body type

Eyes

Hair

Skin

Facial express.

Posture / gait

Grooming

Style / clothes

Accessories

Health

Distinctive features

SPEECH & COMMUNICATION

Languages

Accent

Pitch / timbre

Literacy level

Handwriting

Slang / phrases

Vocal tics & mannerisms

Eye contact

Gestures

Sense of humor

Show or hide emotions?

What are their lying "tells"?

SKILLS, HOBBIES, ACTIVITIES, & GROUPS

Talents / skills

Childhood

Adulthood

Magical gifts

Training

Past jobs

MEMORIES

Earliest

Saddest

Happiest

Scariest

Motivators, wants & goals. What keeps this character going?	
Core vulnerabilities (keep asking "why" to get to the root)	
Personality type(s) and description	

					Love Language(s)	
☐ Introvert	☐ Extrovert	☐ Nervous	☐ Confident	☐ Organized	☐ Careless	☐ Physical Touch
☐ Optimist	☐ Pessimist	☐ Fickle	☐ Constant	☐ Friendly	☐ Challenging	☐ Acts of Service
☐ Thinker	☐ Feeler	☐ Judgemental	☐ Tolerant	☐ Street Smart	☐ Book Smart	☐ Words of Affirmation
☐ Frugal	☐ Lavish	☐ Forgiving	☐ Unforgiving	☐	☐	☐ Quality Time
☐ Curious	☐ Cautious	☐ High Energy	☐ Low Energy	☐	☐	☐ Receiving Gifts

QUESTIONNAIRE

What they assume that is not true:	
What others assume of them that's not true:	
Their stereotype? How do they break it?	
Regrets / things they'd go back & change:	
Biggest fears? (Temporal and inner)	
Secret(s) they carry:	
Lessons learned:	
Hopes (for themselves and/or others):	
Biggest accomplishment(s):	
Duties and obligations:	
The foundations of their moral compass:	
When would they compromise it?	
How do they react to change?	
What do they desire in an ideal partner?	
Who would come to their funeral?	
Favorite secret spot/place to be:	
What they'd rescue from a burning home:	
Important possessions:	
Pet peeves:	

RELATIONSHIPS

Who they depend on for:		Other Characters	Relationship & status to this character
Practical advice			
Mentoring			
Wingman			
Emotional support			
Moral support			
Financial help			
Relationship to **Protagonist:**			
Relationship to **Antagonist:**			

OTHER NAMES (titles, ranks, pseudonyms)

Age (at intro.)

Gender

Group, classification, or species

MC/Protag	Deuteragonist	Antagonist	Secondary	Foil/Contrast	Love Interest	Mentor	Narrator	Confidant	

Birthdate

Birth place

Parents

Education

Ancestry

Social class

Religion

Sexuality

Significant past

Residence

Living with

Occupation

Income

Death?

(attach or sketch image here)

PHYSICAL DESCRIPTION

Body type

Eyes

Hair

Skin

Facial express.

Posture / gait

Grooming

Style / clothes

Accessories

Health

Distinctive features

SPEECH & COMMUNICATION

Languages

Accent

Pitch / timbre

Literacy level

Handwriting

Slang / phrases

Vocal tics & mannerisms

Eye contact

Gestures

Sense of humor

Show or hide emotions?

What are their lying "tells"?

SKILLS, HOBBIES, ACTIVITIES, & GROUPS

Talents / skills

Childhood

Adulthood

Magical gifts

Training

Past jobs

MEMORIES

Earliest

Saddest

Happiest

Scariest

Motivators, wants & goals. What keeps this character going?

Core vulnerabilities (keep asking "why" to get to the root)

Personality type(s) and description

- ☐ Introvert
- ☐ Optimist
- ☐ Thinker
- ☐ Frugal
- ☐ Curious

- ☐ Extrovert
- ☐ Pessimist
- ☐ Feeler
- ☐ Lavish
- ☐ Cautious

- ☐ Nervous
- ☐ Fickle
- ☐ Judgemental
- ☐ Forgiving
- ☐ High Energy

- ☐ Confident
- ☐ Constant
- ☐ Tolerant
- ☐ Unforgiving
- ☐ Low Energy

- ☐ Organized
- ☐ Friendly
- ☐ Street Smart
- ☐
- ☐

- ☐ Careless
- ☐ Challenging
- ☐ Book Smart
- ☐
- ☐

Love Language(s)
- ☐ Physical Touch
- ☐ Acts of Service
- ☐ Words of Affirmation
- ☐ Quality Time
- ☐ Receiving Gifts

QUESTIONNAIRE

What they assume that is not true:

What others assume of them that's not true:

Their stereotype? How do they break it?

Regrets / things they'd go back & change:

Biggest fears? (Temporal and inner)

Secret(s) they carry:

Lessons learned:

Hopes (for themselves and/or others):

Biggest accomplishment(s):

Duties and obligations:

The foundations of their moral compass:

When would they compromise it?

How do they react to change?

What do they desire in an ideal partner?

Who would come to their funeral?

Favorite secret spot/place to be:

What they'd rescue from a burning home:

Important possessions:

Pet peeves:

RELATIONSHIPS

Who they depend on for:		Other Characters	Relationship & status to this character
Practical advice			
Mentoring			
Wingman			
Emotional support			
Moral support			
Financial help			
Relationship to **Protagonist:**			
Relationship to **Antagonist:**			

OTHER NAMES
(titles, ranks,
pseudonyms)

Age (at intro.)

Gender

Group,
classification,
or species

MC/Protag	Deuteragonist	Antagonist	Secondary	Foil/Contrast	Love Interest	Mentor	Narrator	Confidant	

Birthdate

Birth place

Parents

Education

Ancestry

Social class

Religion

Sexuality

Significant
past

Residence

Living with

Occupation

Income

Death?

(attach or sketch image here)

PHYSICAL DESCRIPTION

Body type

Eyes

Hair

Skin

Facial express.

Posture / gait

Grooming

Style / clothes

Accessories

Health

Distinctive
features

SPEECH & COMMUNICATION

Languages

Accent

Pitch / timbre

Literacy level

Handwriting

Slang / phrases

Vocal tics &
mannerisms

Eye contact

Gestures

Sense of
humor

Show or hide
emotions?

What are
their lying
"tells"?

SKILLS, HOBBIES, ACTIVITIES, & GROUPS

Talents / skills

Childhood

Adulthood

Magical gifts

Training

Past jobs

MEMORIES

Earliest

Saddest

Happiest

Scariest

Motivators, wants & goals. What keeps this character going?

Core vulnerabilities (keep asking "why" to get to the root)

Personality type(s) and description

- [ ] Introvert
- [ ] Optimist
- [ ] Thinker
- [ ] Frugal
- [ ] Curious

- [ ] Extrovert
- [ ] Pessimist
- [ ] Feeler
- [ ] Lavish
- [ ] Cautious

- [ ] Nervous
- [ ] Fickle
- [ ] Judgemental
- [ ] Forgiving
- [ ] High Energy

- [ ] Confident
- [ ] Constant
- [ ] Tolerant
- [ ] Unforgiving
- [ ] Low Energy

- [ ] Organized
- [ ] Friendly
- [ ] Street Smart
- [ ]
- [ ]

- [ ] Careless
- [ ] Challenging
- [ ] Book Smart
- [ ]
- [ ]

Love Language(s)
- [ ] Physical Touch
- [ ] Acts of Service
- [ ] Words of Affirmation
- [ ] Quality Time
- [ ] Receiving Gifts

QUESTIONNAIRE

What they assume that is not true:

What others assume of them that's not true:

Their stereotype? How do they break it?

Regrets / things they'd go back & change:

Biggest fears? (Temporal and inner)

Secret(s) they carry:

Lessons learned:

Hopes (for themselves and/or others):

Biggest accomplishment(s):

Duties and obligations:

The foundations of their moral compass:

When would they compromise it?

How do they react to change?

What do they desire in an ideal partner?

Who would come to their funeral?

Favorite secret spot/place to be:

What they'd rescue from a burning home:

Important possessions:

Pet peeves:

RELATIONSHIPS

	Who they depend on for:	Other Characters	Relationship & status to this character
Practical advice			
Mentoring			
Wingman			
Emotional support			
Moral support			
Financial help			
Relationship to **Protagonist:**			
Relationship to **Antagonist:**			

OTHER NAMES (titles, ranks, pseudonyms)

Age (at intro.)

Gender

Group, classification, or species

MC/Protag	Deuteragonist	Antagonist	Secondary	Foil/Contrast	Love Interest	Mentor	Narrator	Confidant	

Birthdate

Birth place

Parents

Education

Ancestry

Social class

Religion

Sexuality

Significant past

Residence

Living with

Occupation

Income

Death?

(attach or sketch image here)

PHYSICAL DESCRIPTION

Body type

Eyes

Hair

Skin

Facial express.

Posture / gait

Grooming

Style / clothes

Accessories

Health

Distinctive features

SPEECH & COMMUNICATION

Languages

Accent

Pitch / timbre

Literacy level

Handwriting

Slang / phrases

Vocal tics & mannerisms

Eye contact

Gestures

Sense of humor

Show or hide emotions?

What are their lying "tells"?

SKILLS, HOBBIES, ACTIVITIES, & GROUPS

Talents / skills

Childhood

Adulthood

Magical gifts

Training

Past jobs

MEMORIES

Earliest

Saddest

Happiest

Scariest

Motivators, wants & goals. What keeps this character going?

Core vulnerabilities (keep asking "why" to get to the root)

Personality type(s) and description

- ☐ Introvert
- ☐ Optimist
- ☐ Thinker
- ☐ Frugal
- ☐ Curious

- ☐ Extrovert
- ☐ Pessimist
- ☐ Feeler
- ☐ Lavish
- ☐ Cautious

- ☐ Nervous
- ☐ Fickle
- ☐ Judgemental
- ☐ Forgiving
- ☐ High Energy

- ☐ Confident
- ☐ Constant
- ☐ Tolerant
- ☐ Unforgiving
- ☐ Low Energy

- ☐ Organized
- ☐ Friendly
- ☐ Street Smart
- ☐
- ☐

- ☐ Careless
- ☐ Challenging
- ☐ Book Smart
- ☐
- ☐

Love Language(s)
- ☐ Physical Touch
- ☐ Acts of Service
- ☐ Words of Affirmation
- ☐ Quality Time
- ☐ Receiving Gifts

QUESTIONNAIRE

What they assume that is not true:

What others assume of them that's not true:

Their stereotype? How do they break it?

Regrets / things they'd go back & change:

Biggest fears? (Temporal and inner)

Secret(s) they carry:

Lessons learned:

Hopes (for themselves and/or others):

Biggest accomplishment(s):

Duties and obligations:

The foundations of their moral compass:

When would they compromise it?

How do they react to change?

What do they desire in an ideal partner?

Who would come to their funeral?

Favorite secret spot/place to be:

What they'd rescue from a burning home:

Important possessions:

Pet peeves:

RELATIONSHIPS

Who they depend on for:		Other Characters	Relationship & status to this character
Practical advice			
Mentoring			
Wingman			
Emotional support			
Moral support			
Financial help			
Relationship to **Protagonist:**			
Relationship to **Antagonist:**			

OTHER NAMES
(titles, ranks,
pseudonyms)

Age (at intro.)

Gender

Group,
classification,
or species

MC/Protag	Deuteragonist	Antagonist	Secondary	Foil/Contrast	Love Interest	Mentor	Narrator	Confidant	

Birthdate

Birth place

Parents

Education

Ancestry

Social class

Religion

Sexuality

Significant past

Residence

Living with

Occupation

Income

Death?

(attach or sketch image here)

PHYSICAL DESCRIPTION

Body type

Eyes

Hair

Skin

Facial express.

Posture / gait

Grooming

Style / clothes

Accessories

Health

Distinctive features

SPEECH & COMMUNICATION

Languages

Accent

Pitch / timbre

Literacy level

Handwriting

Slang / phrases

Vocal tics & mannerisms

Eye contact

Gestures

Sense of humor

Show or hide emotions?

What are their lying "tells"?

SKILLS, HOBBIES, ACTIVITIES, & GROUPS

Talents / skills

Childhood

Adulthood

Magical gifts

Training

Past jobs

MEMORIES

Earliest

Saddest

Happiest

Scariest

Motivators, wants & goals. What keeps this character going?

Core vulnerabilities (keep asking "why" to get to the root)

Personality type(s) and description

- [ ] Introvert
- [ ] Optimist
- [ ] Thinker
- [ ] Frugal
- [ ] Curious

- [ ] Extrovert
- [ ] Pessimist
- [ ] Feeler
- [ ] Lavish
- [ ] Cautious

- [ ] Nervous
- [ ] Fickle
- [ ] Judgemental
- [ ] Forgiving
- [ ] High Energy

- [ ] Confident
- [ ] Constant
- [ ] Tolerant
- [ ] Unforgiving
- [ ] Low Energy

- [ ] Organized
- [ ] Friendly
- [ ] Street Smart
- [ ]
- [ ]

- [ ] Careless
- [ ] Challenging
- [ ] Book Smart
- [ ]
- [ ]

Love Language(s)
- [ ] Physical Touch
- [ ] Acts of Service
- [ ] Words of Affirmation
- [ ] Quality Time
- [ ] Receiving Gifts

QUESTIONNAIRE

What they assume that is not true:

What others assume of them that's not true:

Their stereotype? How do they break it?

Regrets / things they'd go back & change:

Biggest fears? (Temporal and inner)

Secret(s) they carry:

Lessons learned:

Hopes (for themselves and/or others):

Biggest accomplishment(s):

Duties and obligations:

The foundations of their moral compass:

When would they compromise it?

How do they react to change?

What do they desire in an ideal partner?

Who would come to their funeral?

Favorite secret spot/place to be:

What they'd rescue from a burning home:

Important possessions:

Pet peeves:

RELATIONSHIPS

	Who they depend on for:	Other Characters	Relationship & status to this character
Practical advice			
Mentoring			
Wingman			
Emotional support			
Moral support			
Financial help			
Relationship to **Protagonist:**			
Relationship to **Antagonist:**			

OTHER NAMES
(titles, ranks, pseudonyms)

Age (at intro.)

Gender

Group, classification, or species

MC/Protag	Deuteragonist	Antagonist	Secondary	Foil/Contrast	Love Interest	Mentor	Narrator	Confidant	

Birthdate

Birth place

Parents

Education

Ancestry

Social class

Religion

Sexuality

Significant past

Residence

Living with

Occupation

Income

Death?

(attach or sketch image here)

PHYSICAL DESCRIPTION

Body type

Eyes

Hair

Skin

Facial express.

Posture / gait

Grooming

Style / clothes

Accessories

Health

Distinctive features

SPEECH & COMMUNICATION

Languages

Accent

Pitch / timbre

Literacy level

Handwriting

Slang / phrases

Vocal tics & mannerisms

Eye contact

Gestures

Sense of humor

Show or hide emotions?

What are their lying "tells"?

SKILLS, HOBBIES, ACTIVITIES, & GROUPS

Talents / skills

Childhood

Adulthood

Magical gifts

Training

Past jobs

MEMORIES

Earliest

Saddest

Happiest

Scariest

Motivators, wants & goals. What keeps this character going?

Core vulnerabilities (keep asking "why" to get to the root)

Personality type(s) and description

- [ ] Introvert
- [ ] Optimist
- [ ] Thinker
- [ ] Frugal
- [ ] Curious

- [ ] Extrovert
- [ ] Pessimist
- [ ] Feeler
- [ ] Lavish
- [ ] Cautious

- [ ] Nervous
- [ ] Fickle
- [ ] Judgemental
- [ ] Forgiving
- [ ] High Energy

- [ ] Confident
- [ ] Constant
- [ ] Tolerant
- [ ] Unforgiving
- [ ] Low Energy

- [ ] Organized
- [ ] Friendly
- [ ] Street Smart
- [ ]
- [ ]

- [ ] Careless
- [ ] Challenging
- [ ] Book Smart
- [ ]
- [ ]

Love Language(s)
- [ ] Physical Touch
- [ ] Acts of Service
- [ ] Words of Affirmation
- [ ] Quality Time
- [ ] Receiving Gifts

QUESTIONNAIRE

What they assume that is not true:
What others assume of them that's not true:
Their stereotype? How do they break it?

Regrets / things they'd go back & change:
Biggest fears? (Temporal and inner)
Secret(s) they carry:
Lessons learned:
Hopes (for themselves and/or others):
Biggest accomplishment(s):
Duties and obligations:

The foundations of their moral compass:
When would they compromise it?

How do they react to change?
What do they desire in an ideal partner?
Who would come to their funeral?
Favorite secret spot/place to be:
What they'd rescue from a burning home:
Important possessions:
Pet peeves:

RELATIONSHIPS

Who they depend on for:		Other Characters	Relationship & status to this character
Practical advice			
Mentoring			
Wingman			
Emotional support			
Moral support			
Financial help			
Relationship to **Protagonist:**			
Relationship to **Antagonist:**			

OTHER NAMES
(titles, ranks,
pseudonyms)

Age (at intro.)

Gender

Group,
classification,
or species

MC/Protag	Deuteragonist	Antagonist	Secondary	Foil/Contrast	Love Interest	Mentor	Narrator	Confidant	

Birthdate

Birth place

Parents

Education

Ancestry

Social class

Religion

Sexuality

Significant
past

Residence

Living with

Occupation

Income

Death?

(attach or sketch image here)

PHYSICAL DESCRIPTION

Body type

Eyes

Hair

Skin

Facial express.

Posture / gait

Grooming

Style / clothes

Accessories

Health

Distinctive
features

SPEECH & COMMUNICATION

Languages

Accent

Pitch / timbre

Literacy level

Handwriting

Slang / phrases

Vocal tics &
mannerisms

Eye contact

Gestures

Sense of
humor

Show or hide
emotions?

What are
their lying
"tells"?

SKILLS, HOBBIES, ACTIVITIES, & GROUPS

Talents / skills

Childhood

Adulthood

Magical gifts

Training

Past jobs

MEMORIES

Earliest

Saddest

Happiest

Scariest

Motivators, wants & goals. What keeps this character going?

Core vulnerabilities (keep asking "why" to get to the root)

Personality type(s) and description

- [ ] Introvert
- [ ] Optimist
- [ ] Thinker
- [ ] Frugal
- [ ] Curious

- [ ] Extrovert
- [ ] Pessimist
- [ ] Feeler
- [ ] Lavish
- [ ] Cautious

- [ ] Nervous
- [ ] Fickle
- [ ] Judgemental
- [ ] Forgiving
- [ ] High Energy

- [ ] Confident
- [ ] Constant
- [ ] Tolerant
- [ ] Unforgiving
- [ ] Low Energy

- [ ] Organized
- [ ] Friendly
- [ ] Street Smart
- [ ]
- [ ]

- [ ] Careless
- [ ] Challenging
- [ ] Book Smart
- [ ]
- [ ]

Love Language(s)
- [ ] Physical Touch
- [ ] Acts of Service
- [ ] Words of Affirmation
- [ ] Quality Time
- [ ] Receiving Gifts

QUESTIONNAIRE

What they assume that is not true:

What others assume of them that's not true:

Their stereotype? How do they break it?

Regrets / things they'd go back & change:

Biggest fears? (Temporal and inner)

Secret(s) they carry:

Lessons learned:

Hopes (for themselves and/or others):

Biggest accomplishment(s):

Duties and obligations:

The foundations of their moral compass:

When would they compromise it?

How do they react to change?

What do they desire in an ideal partner?

Who would come to their funeral?

Favorite secret spot/place to be:

What they'd rescue from a burning home:

Important possessions:

Pet peeves:

RELATIONSHIPS

Who they depend on for:		Other Characters	Relationship & status to this character
Practical advice			
Mentoring			
Wingman			
Emotional support			
Moral support			
Financial help			
Relationship to **Protagonist:**			
Relationship to **Antagonist:**			

OTHER NAMES
(titles, ranks,
pseudonyms)

Age (at intro.)

Gender

Group,
classification,
or species

MC/Protag	Deuteragonist	Antagonist	Secondary	Foil/Contrast	Love Interest	Mentor	Narrator	Confidant	

Birthdate

Birth place

Parents

Education

Ancestry

Social class

Religion

Sexuality

Significant past

Residence

Living with

Occupation

Income

Death?

(attach or sketch image here)

PHYSICAL DESCRIPTION

Body type

Eyes

Hair

Skin

Facial express.

Posture / gait

Grooming

Style / clothes

Accessories

Health

Distinctive features

SPEECH & COMMUNICATION

Languages

Accent

Pitch / timbre

Literacy level

Handwriting

Slang / phrases

Vocal tics & mannerisms

Eye contact

Gestures

Sense of humor

Show or hide emotions?

What are their lying "tells"?

SKILLS, HOBBIES, ACTIVITIES, & GROUPS

Talents / skills

Childhood

Adulthood

Magical gifts

Training

Past jobs

MEMORIES

Earliest

Saddest

Happiest

Scariest

Motivators, wants & goals. What keeps this character going?

Core vulnerabilities (keep asking "why" to get to the root)

Personality type(s) and description

- [ ] Introvert
- [ ] Optimist
- [ ] Thinker
- [ ] Frugal
- [ ] Curious

- [ ] Extrovert
- [ ] Pessimist
- [ ] Feeler
- [ ] Lavish
- [ ] Cautious

- [ ] Nervous
- [ ] Fickle
- [ ] Judgemental
- [ ] Forgiving
- [ ] High Energy

- [ ] Confident
- [ ] Constant
- [ ] Tolerant
- [ ] Unforgiving
- [ ] Low Energy

- [ ] Organized
- [ ] Friendly
- [ ] Street Smart
- [ ]
- [ ]

- [ ] Careless
- [ ] Challenging
- [ ] Book Smart
- [ ]
- [ ]

Love Language(s)
- [ ] Physical Touch
- [ ] Acts of Service
- [ ] Words of Affirmation
- [ ] Quality Time
- [ ] Receiving Gifts

QUESTIONNAIRE

What they assume that is not true:

What others assume of them that's not true:

Their stereotype? How do they break it?

Regrets / things they'd go back & change:

Biggest fears? (Temporal and inner)

Secret(s) they carry:

Lessons learned:

Hopes (for themselves and/or others):

Biggest accomplishment(s):

Duties and obligations:

The foundations of their moral compass:

When would they compromise it?

How do they react to change?

What do they desire in an ideal partner?

Who would come to their funeral?

Favorite secret spot/place to be:

What they'd rescue from a burning home:

Important possessions:

Pet peeves:

RELATIONSHIPS

Who they depend on for:		Other Characters	Relationship & status to this character
Practical advice			
Mentoring			
Wingman			
Emotional support			
Moral support			
Financial help			
Relationship to **Protagonist:**			
Relationship to **Antagonist:**			

42 CHARACTER

OTHER NAMES
(titles, ranks, pseudonyms)

Age (at intro.)

Gender

Group, classification, or species

MC/Protag	Deuteragonist	Antagonist	Secondary	Foil/Contrast	Love Interest	Mentor	Narrator	Confidant	

Birthdate

Birth place

Parents

Education

Ancestry

Social class

Religion

Sexuality

Significant past

Residence

Living with

Occupation

Income

Death?

(attach or sketch image here)

PHYSICAL DESCRIPTION

Body type

Eyes

Hair

Skin

Facial express.

Posture / gait

Grooming

Style / clothes

Accessories

Health

Distinctive features

SPEECH & COMMUNICATION

Languages

Accent

Pitch / timbre

Literacy level

Handwriting

Slang / phrases

Vocal tics & mannerisms

Eye contact

Gestures

Sense of humor

Show or hide emotions?

What are their lying "tells"?

SKILLS, HOBBIES, ACTIVITIES, & GROUPS

Talents / skills

Childhood

Adulthood

Magical gifts

Training

Past jobs

MEMORIES

Earliest

Saddest

Happiest

Scariest

Motivators, wants & goals. What keeps this character going?

Core vulnerabilities (keep asking "why" to get to the root)

Personality type(s) and description

- ☐ Introvert
- ☐ Optimist
- ☐ Thinker
- ☐ Frugal
- ☐ Curious

- ☐ Extrovert
- ☐ Pessimist
- ☐ Feeler
- ☐ Lavish
- ☐ Cautious

- ☐ Nervous
- ☐ Fickle
- ☐ Judgemental
- ☐ Forgiving
- ☐ High Energy

- ☐ Confident
- ☐ Constant
- ☐ Tolerant
- ☐ Unforgiving
- ☐ Low Energy

- ☐ Organized
- ☐ Friendly
- ☐ Street Smart
- ☐
- ☐

- ☐ Careless
- ☐ Challenging
- ☐ Book Smart
- ☐
- ☐

Love Language(s)
- ☐ Physical Touch
- ☐ Acts of Service
- ☐ Words of Affirmation
- ☐ Quality Time
- ☐ Receiving Gifts

QUESTIONNAIRE

What they assume that is not true:

What others assume of them that's not true:

Their stereotype? How do they break it?

Regrets / things they'd go back & change:

Biggest fears? (Temporal and inner)

Secret(s) they carry:

Lessons learned:

Hopes (for themselves and/or others):

Biggest accomplishment(s):

Duties and obligations:

The foundations of their moral compass:

When would they compromise it?

How do they react to change?

What do they desire in an ideal partner?

Who would come to their funeral?

Favorite secret spot/place to be:

What they'd rescue from a burning home:

Important possessions:

Pet peeves:

RELATIONSHIPS

Who they depend on for:		Other Characters	Relationship & status to this character
Practical advice			
Mentoring			
Wingman			
Emotional support			
Moral support			
Financial help			
Relationship to **Protagonist:**			
Relationship to **Antagonist:**			

OTHER NAMES
(titles, ranks, pseudonyms)

Age (at intro.)

Gender

Group, classification, or species

MC/Protag	Deuteragonist	Antagonist	Secondary	Foil/Contrast	Love Interest	Mentor	Narrator	Confidant	

Birthdate

Birth place

Parents

Education

Ancestry

Social class

Religion

Sexuality

Significant past

Residence

Living with

Occupation

Income

Death?

(attach or sketch image here)

PHYSICAL DESCRIPTION

Body type

Eyes

Hair

Skin

Facial express.

Posture / gait

Grooming

Style / clothes

Accessories

Health

Distinctive features

SPEECH & COMMUNICATION

Languages

Accent

Pitch / timbre

Literacy level

Handwriting

Slang / phrases

Vocal tics & mannerisms

Eye contact

Gestures

Sense of humor

Show or hide emotions?

What are their lying "tells"?

SKILLS, HOBBIES, ACTIVITIES, & GROUPS

Talents / skills

Childhood

Adulthood

Magical gifts

Training

Past jobs

MEMORIES

Earliest

Saddest

Happiest

Scariest

Motivators, wants & goals. What keeps this character going?

Core vulnerabilities (keep asking "why" to get to the root)

Personality type(s) and description

- [ ] Introvert
- [ ] Optimist
- [ ] Thinker
- [ ] Frugal
- [ ] Curious

- [ ] Extrovert
- [ ] Pessimist
- [ ] Feeler
- [ ] Lavish
- [ ] Cautious

- [ ] Nervous
- [ ] Fickle
- [ ] Judgemental
- [ ] Forgiving
- [ ] High Energy

- [ ] Confident
- [ ] Constant
- [ ] Tolerant
- [ ] Unforgiving
- [ ] Low Energy

- [ ] Organized
- [ ] Friendly
- [ ] Street Smart
- [ ]
- [ ]

- [ ] Careless
- [ ] Challenging
- [ ] Book Smart
- [ ]
- [ ]

Love Language(s)
- [ ] Physical Touch
- [ ] Acts of Service
- [ ] Words of Affirmation
- [ ] Quality Time
- [ ] Receiving Gifts

QUESTIONNAIRE

What they assume that is not true:

What others assume of them that's not true:

Their stereotype? How do they break it?

Regrets / things they'd go back & change:

Biggest fears? (Temporal and inner)

Secret(s) they carry:

Lessons learned:

Hopes (for themselves and/or others):

Biggest accomplishment(s):

Duties and obligations:

The foundations of their moral compass:

When would they compromise it?

How do they react to change?

What do they desire in an ideal partner?

Who would come to their funeral?

Favorite secret spot/place to be:

What they'd rescue from a burning home:

Important possessions:

Pet peeves:

RELATIONSHIPS

Who they depend on for:		Other Characters	Relationship & status to this character
Practical advice			
Mentoring			
Wingman			
Emotional support			
Moral support			
Financial help			
Relationship to **Protagonist:**			
Relationship to **Antagonist:**			

CHARACTER

OTHER NAMES
(titles, ranks,
pseudonyms)

Age (at intro.)

Gender

Group,
classification,
or species

MC/Protag	Deuteragonist	Antagonist	Secondary	Foil/Contrast	Love Interest	Mentor	Narrator	Confidant	

Birthdate

Birth place

Parents

Education

Ancestry

Social class

Religion

Sexuality

Significant past

Residence

Living with

Occupation

Income

Death?

(attach or sketch image here)

PHYSICAL DESCRIPTION

Body type

Eyes

Hair

Skin

Facial express.

Posture / gait

Grooming

Style / clothes

Accessories

Health

Distinctive features

SPEECH & COMMUNICATION

Languages

Accent

Pitch / timbre

Literacy level

Handwriting

Slang / phrases

Vocal tics & mannerisms

Eye contact

Gestures

Sense of humor

Show or hide emotions?

What are their lying "tells"?

SKILLS, HOBBIES, ACTIVITIES, & GROUPS

Talents / skills

Childhood

Adulthood

Magical gifts

Training

Past jobs

MEMORIES

Earliest

Saddest

Happiest

Scariest

Motivators, wants & goals. What keeps this character going?	
Core vulnerabilities (keep asking "why" to get to the root)	
Personality type(s) and description	

						Love Language(s)	
☐ Introvert	☐ Extrovert	☐ Nervous	☐ Confident	☐ Organized	☐ Careless		☐ Physical Touch
☐ Optimist	☐ Pessimist	☐ Fickle	☐ Constant	☐ Friendly	☐ Challenging		☐ Acts of Service
☐ Thinker	☐ Feeler	☐ Judgemental	☐ Tolerant	☐ Street Smart	☐ Book Smart		☐ Words of Affirmation
☐ Frugal	☐ Lavish	☐ Forgiving	☐ Unforgiving	☐	☐		☐ Quality Time
☐ Curious	☐ Cautious	☐ High Energy	☐ Low Energy	☐	☐		☐ Receiving Gifts

QUESTIONNAIRE

What they assume that is not true:

What others assume of them that's not true:

Their stereotype? How do they break it?

Regrets / things they'd go back & change:

Biggest fears? (Temporal and inner)

Secret(s) they carry:

Lessons learned:

Hopes (for themselves and/or others):

Biggest accomplishment(s):

Duties and obligations:

The foundations of their moral compass:

When would they compromise it?

How do they react to change?

What do they desire in an ideal partner?

Who would come to their funeral?

Favorite secret spot/place to be:

What they'd rescue from a burning home:

Important possessions:

Pet peeves:

RELATIONSHIPS

Who they depend on for:		Other Characters	Relationship & status to this character
Practical advice			
Mentoring			
Wingman			
Emotional support			
Moral support			
Financial help			
Relationship to **Protagonist:**			
Relationship to **Antagonist:**			

OTHER NAMES
(titles, ranks,
pseudonyms)

Age (at intro.)

Gender

Group,
classification,
or species

MC/Protag	Deuteragonist	Antagonist	Secondary	Foil/Contrast	Love Interest	Mentor	Narrator	Confidant	

Birthdate

Birth place

Parents

Education

Ancestry

Social class

Religion

Sexuality

Significant past

Residence

Living with

Occupation

Income

Death?

(attach or sketch image here)

PHYSICAL DESCRIPTION

Body type

Eyes

Hair

Skin

Facial express.

Posture / gait

Grooming

Style / clothes

Accessories

Health

Distinctive features

SPEECH & COMMUNICATION

Languages

Accent

Pitch / timbre

Literacy level

Handwriting

Slang / phrases

Vocal tics & mannerisms

Eye contact

Gestures

Sense of humor

Show or hide emotions?

What are their lying "tells"?

SKILLS, HOBBIES, ACTIVITIES, & GROUPS

Talents / skills

Childhood

Adulthood

Magical gifts

Training

Past jobs

MEMORIES

Earliest

Saddest

Happiest

Scariest

Motivators, wants &
goals. What keeps
this character going?

Core vulnerabilities
(keep asking "why" to
get to the root)

Personality type(s)
and description

- [ ] Introvert
- [ ] Optimist
- [ ] Thinker
- [ ] Frugal
- [ ] Curious

- [ ] Extrovert
- [ ] Pessimist
- [ ] Feeler
- [ ] Lavish
- [ ] Cautious

- [ ] Nervous
- [ ] Fickle
- [ ] Judgemental
- [ ] Forgiving
- [ ] High Energy

- [ ] Confident
- [ ] Constant
- [ ] Tolerant
- [ ] Unforgiving
- [ ] Low Energy

- [ ] Organized
- [ ] Friendly
- [ ] Street Smart
- [ ]
- [ ]

- [ ] Careless
- [ ] Challenging
- [ ] Book Smart
- [ ]
- [ ]

Love Language(s)

- [ ] Physical Touch
- [ ] Acts of Service
- [ ] Words of Affirmation
- [ ] Quality Time
- [ ] Receiving Gifts

QUESTIONNAIRE

What they assume that is not true:

What others assume of them that's not true:

Their stereotype? How do they break it?

Regrets / things they'd go back & change:

Biggest fears? (Temporal and inner)

Secret(s) they carry:

Lessons learned:

Hopes (for themselves and/or others):

Biggest accomplishment(s):

Duties and obligations:

The foundations of their moral compass:

When would they compromise it?

How do they react to change?

What do they desire in an ideal partner?

Who would come to their funeral?

Favorite secret spot/place to be:

What they'd rescue from a burning home:

Important possessions:

Pet peeves:

RELATIONSHIPS

Who they depend on for:		Other Characters	Relationship & status to this character
Practical advice			
Mentoring			
Wingman			
Emotional support			
Moral support			
Financial help			
Relationship to **Protagonist:**			
Relationship to **Antagonist:**			

SECONDARY CHARACTERS

"A lone protagonist never receives as great a reaction as one with a well-developed supporting cast. Foils serve to reinforce and highlight the hero's good (and bad) characteristics, and also give the protagonist a chance to shine outside the primary narrative."

— Susan Spann, *Dr. Watson, I Presume? The Importance of Killer Sidekicks*

SECONDARY CHARACTER

OTHER NAMES
(including titles, ranks, pseudonyms)

Age (at intro.)

Gender

Group, classification or species

Birthdate

Birth place

Parents

Education

Ancestry

Social class

Religion

Sexuality

Significant past

Residence

Living with

Death?

Occupation

Income

(attach or sketch image here)

PHYSICAL DESCRIPTION & COMMUNICATION

Body type

Eyes

Hair

Skin

Facial express.

Posture / gait

Grooming

Style / clothes

Accessories

Health

Noted features

Language(s)

Voice & accent

Literacy level

Handwriting

Eye contact

Gestures

Sense of humor

Show emotion?

Lying "tells"

Mannerisms and tics

PERSONALITY

Motivators

Personality type

Vulnerabilities

Love language

QUESTIONNAIRE

Strengths / skills

Magical gifts

Weaknesses

Obligations

Accomplish.

Secrets

Fears

Hopes

Importants

Regrets

What do they assume that is not true?

What do others assume about them that's not true?

What is their stereotype? How do they break it?

Moral compass? When would they compromise?

How do they react to change?

PLOT PURPOSE

SECONDARY CHARACTER

OTHER NAMES (including titles, ranks, pseudonyms)

Age (at intro.)

Gender

Group, classification or species

Birthdate

Birth place

Parents

Education

Ancestry

Social class

Religion

Sexuality

Significant past

Residence

Living with

Occupation

Income

Death?

(attach or sketch image here)

PHYSICAL DESCRIPTION & COMMUNICATION

Body type	Language(s)
Eyes	Voice & accent
Hair	Literacy level
Skin	Handwriting
Facial express.	Eye contact
Posture / gait	Gestures
Grooming	Sense of humor
Style / clothes	Show emotion?
Accessories	Lying "tells"
Health	Mannerisms and tics
Noted features	

PERSONALITY

Motivators

Vulnerabilities

Personality type

Love language

QUESTIONNAIRE

Strengths / skills	Secrets
Magical gifts	Fears
Weaknesses	Hopes
Obligations	Importants
Accomplish.	Regrets

What do they assume that is not true?

What do others assume about them that's not true?

What is their stereotype? How do they break it?

Moral compass? When would they compromise?

How do they react to change?

PLOT PURPOSE

SECONDARY CHARACTER

OTHER NAMES
(including titles, ranks, pseudonyms)

Age (at intro.)

Gender

Group, classification or species

Birthdate

Birth place

Parents

Education

Ancestry

Social class

Religion

Sexuality

Significant past

Residence

Living with

Occupation

Income

Death?

(attach or sketch image here)

PHYSICAL DESCRIPTION & COMMUNICATION

Body type

Eyes

Hair

Skin

Facial express.

Posture / gait

Grooming

Style / clothes

Accessories

Health

Noted features

Language(s)

Voice & accent

Literacy level

Handwriting

Eye contact

Gestures

Sense of humor

Show emotion?

Lying "tells"

Mannerisms and tics

PERSONALITY

Motivators

Personality type

Vulnerabilities

Love language

QUESTIONNAIRE

Strengths / skills

Magical gifts

Weaknesses

Obligations

Accomplish.

Secrets

Fears

Hopes

Importants

Regrets

What do they assume that is not true?

What do others assume about them that's not true?

What is their stereotype? How do they break it?

Moral compass? When would they compromise?

How do they react to change?

PLOT PURPOSE

SECONDARY CHARACTER

OTHER NAMES (including titles, ranks, pseudonyms)

Age (at intro.)

Gender

Group, classification or species

Birthdate

Birth place

Parents

Education

Ancestry

Social class

Religion

Sexuality

Significant past

Residence

Living with

Occupation

Income

Death?

(attach or sketch image here)

PHYSICAL DESCRIPTION & COMMUNICATION

Body type

Eyes

Hair

Skin

Facial express.

Posture / gait

Grooming

Style / clothes

Accessories

Health

Noted features

Language(s)

Voice & accent

Literacy level

Handwriting

Eye contact

Gestures

Sense of humor

Show emotion?

Lying "tells"

Mannerisms and tics

PERSONALITY

Motivators

Personality type

Vulnerabilities

Love language

QUESTIONNAIRE

Strengths / skills

Magical gifts

Weaknesses

Obligations

Accomplish.

Secrets

Fears

Hopes

Importants

Regrets

What do they assume that is not true?

What do others assume about them that's not true?

What is their stereotype? How do they break it?

Moral compass? When would they compromise?

How do they react to change?

PLOT PURPOSE

SECONDARY CHARACTER

OTHER NAMES (including titles, ranks, pseudonyms)

Age (at intro.)

Gender

Group, classification or species

Birthdate

Birth place

Parents

Education

Ancestry

Social class

Religion

Sexuality

Significant past

Residence

Living with

Occupation

Income

Death?

(attach or sketch image here)

PHYSICAL DESCRIPTION & COMMUNICATION

Body type

Eyes

Hair

Skin

Facial express.

Posture / gait

Grooming

Style / clothes

Accessories

Health

Noted features

Language(s)

Voice & accent

Literacy level

Handwriting

Eye contact

Gestures

Sense of humor

Show emotion?

Lying "tells"

Mannerisms and tics

PERSONALITY

Motivators

Personality type

Vulnerabilities

Love language

QUESTIONNAIRE

Strengths / skills

Magical gifts

Weaknesses

Obligations

Accomplish.

Secrets

Fears

Hopes

Importants

Regrets

What do they assume that is not true?

What do others assume about them that's not true?

What is their stereotype? How do they break it?

Moral compass? When would they compromise?

How do they react to change?

PLOT PURPOSE

SECONDARY CHARACTER

OTHER NAMES (including titles, ranks, pseudonyms)

Age (at intro.)

Gender

Group, classification or species

Birthdate

Birth place

Parents

Education

Ancestry

Social class

Religion

Sexuality

Significant past

Residence

Living with

Occupation

Income

Death?

(attach or sketch image here)

PHYSICAL DESCRIPTION & COMMUNICATION

Body type

Eyes

Hair

Skin

Facial express.

Posture / gait

Grooming

Style / clothes

Accessories

Health

Noted features

Language(s)

Voice & accent

Literacy level

Handwriting

Eye contact

Gestures

Sense of humor

Show emotion?

Lying "tells"

Mannerisms and tics

PERSONALITY

Motivators

Personality type

Vulnerabilities

Love language

QUESTIONNAIRE

Strengths / skills

Magical gifts

Weaknesses

Obligations

Accomplish.

Secrets

Fears

Hopes

Importants

Regrets

What do they assume that is not true?

What do others assume about them that's not true?

What is their stereotype? How do they break it?

Moral compass? When would they compromise?

How do they react to change?

PLOT PURPOSE

SECONDARY CHARACTER

OTHER NAMES (including titles, ranks, pseudonyms)

Age (at intro.)

Gender

Group, classification or species

Birthdate

Birth place

Parents

Education

Ancestry

Social class

Religion

Sexuality

Significant past

Residence

Living with

Occupation

Income

Death?

(attach or sketch image here)

PHYSICAL DESCRIPTION & COMMUNICATION

Body type

Eyes

Hair

Skin

Facial express.

Posture / gait

Grooming

Style / clothes

Accessories

Health

Noted features

Language(s)

Voice & accent

Literacy level

Handwriting

Eye contact

Gestures

Sense of humor

Show emotion?

Lying "tells"

Mannerisms and tics

PERSONALITY

Motivators

Personality type

Vulnerabilities

Love language

QUESTIONNAIRE

Strengths / skills

Magical gifts

Weaknesses

Obligations

Accomplish.

Secrets

Fears

Hopes

Importants

Regrets

What do they assume that is not true?

What do others assume about them that's not true?

What is their stereotype? How do they break it?

Moral compass? When would they compromise?

How do they react to change?

PLOT PURPOSE

SECONDARY CHARACTER

OTHER NAMES (including titles, ranks, pseudonyms)

Age (at intro.)

Gender

Group, classification or species

Birthdate

Birth place

Parents

Education

Ancestry

Social class

Religion

Sexuality

Significant past

Residence

Living with

Occupation

Income

Death?

(attach or sketch image here)

PHYSICAL DESCRIPTION & COMMUNICATION

Body type

Eyes

Hair

Skin

Facial express.

Posture / gait

Grooming

Style / clothes

Accessories

Health

Noted features

Language(s)

Voice & accent

Literacy level

Handwriting

Eye contact

Gestures

Sense of humor

Show emotion?

Lying "tells"

Mannerisms and tics

PERSONALITY

Motivators

Personality type

Vulnerabilities

Love language

QUESTIONNAIRE

Strengths / skills

Magical gifts

Weaknesses

Obligations

Accomplish.

Secrets

Fears

Hopes

Importants

Regrets

What do they assume that is not true?

What do others assume about them that's not true?

What is their stereotype? How do they break it?

Moral compass? When would they compromise?

How do they react to change?

PLOT PURPOSE

SECONDARY CHARACTER

OTHER NAMES
(including titles, ranks, pseudonyms)

Age (at intro.)

Gender

Group, classification or species

Birthdate	Ancestry
Birth place	Social class
Parents	Religion
Education	Sexuality

Significant past

Residence	Occupation
Living with	Income

Death?

(attach or sketch image here)

PHYSICAL DESCRIPTION & COMMUNICATION

Body type	Language(s)
Eyes	Voice & accent
Hair	Literacy level
Skin	Handwriting
Facial express.	Eye contact
Posture / gait	Gestures
Grooming	Sense of humor
Style / clothes	Show emotion?
Accessories	Lying "tells"
Health	Mannerisms and tics
Noted features	

PERSONALITY

Motivators	Vulnerabilities
Personality type	Love language

QUESTIONNAIRE

Strengths / skills	Secrets
Magical gifts	Fears
Weaknesses	Hopes
Obligations	Importants
Accomplish.	Regrets

What do they assume that is not true?

What do others assume about them that's not true?

What is their stereotype? How do they break it?

Moral compass? When would they compromise?

How do they react to change?

PLOT PURPOSE

SECONDARY CHARACTER

OTHER NAMES
(including titles, ranks, pseudonyms)

Age (at intro.)

Gender

Group, classification or species

Birthdate

Birth place

Parents

Education

Ancestry

Social class

Religion

Sexuality

Significant past

Residence

Living with

Occupation

Income

Death?

(attach or sketch image here)

PHYSICAL DESCRIPTION & COMMUNICATION

Body type

Eyes

Hair

Skin

Facial express.

Posture / gait

Grooming

Style / clothes

Accessories

Health

Noted features

Language(s)

Voice & accent

Literacy level

Handwriting

Eye contact

Gestures

Sense of humor

Show emotion?

Lying "tells"

Mannerisms and tics

PERSONALITY

Motivators

Personality type

Vulnerabilities

Love language

QUESTIONNAIRE

Strengths / skills

Magical gifts

Weaknesses

Obligations

Accomplish.

Secrets

Fears

Hopes

Importants

Regrets

What do they assume that is not true?

What do others assume about them that's not true?

What is their stereotype? How do they break it?

Moral compass? When would they compromise?

How do they react to change?

PLOT PURPOSE

SECONDARY CHARACTER

OTHER NAMES (including titles, ranks, pseudonyms)

Age (at intro.)

Gender

Group, classification or species

Birthdate

Birth place

Parents

Education

Ancestry

Social class

Religion

Sexuality

Significant past

Residence

Living with

Occupation

Income

Death?

(attach or sketch image here)

PHYSICAL DESCRIPTION & COMMUNICATION

Body type

Eyes

Hair

Skin

Facial express.

Posture / gait

Grooming

Style / clothes

Accessories

Health

Noted features

Language(s)

Voice & accent

Literacy level

Handwriting

Eye contact

Gestures

Sense of humor

Show emotion?

Lying "tells"

Mannerisms and tics

PERSONALITY

Motivators

Personality type

Vulnerabilities

Love language

QUESTIONNAIRE

Strengths / skills

Magical gifts

Weaknesses

Obligations

Accomplish.

Secrets

Fears

Hopes

Importants

Regrets

What do they assume that is not true?

What do others assume about them that's not true?

What is their stereotype? How do they break it?

Moral compass? When would they compromise?

How do they react to change?

PLOT PURPOSE

SECONDARY CHARACTER

OTHER NAMES
(including
titles, ranks,
pseudonyms)

Age (at intro.)

Gender

Group,
classification
or species

Birthdate
Birth place
Parents
Education

Ancestry
Social class
Religion
Sexuality

Significant
past

Residence
Living with

Occupation
Income

Death?

(attach or sketch image here)

PHYSICAL DESCRIPTION & COMMUNICATION

Body type
Eyes
Hair
Skin
Facial express.
Posture / gait
Grooming
Style / clothes
Accessories
Health
Noted features

Language(s)
Voice & accent
Literacy level
Handwriting
Eye contact
Gestures
Sense of humor
Show emotion?
Lying "tells"
Mannerisms
and tics

PERSONALITY

Motivators

Personality type

Vulnerabilities

Love language

QUESTIONNAIRE

Strengths / skills
Magical gifts
Weaknesses
Obligations
Accomplish.

Secrets
Fears
Hopes
Importants
Regrets

What do they assume that is
not true?

What do others assume
about them that's not true?

What is their stereotype?
How do they break it?

Moral compass? When
would they compromise?

How do they react to
change?

PLOT PURPOSE

SECONDARY CHARACTER

OTHER NAMES (including titles, ranks, pseudonyms)

Age (at intro.)

Gender

Group, classification or species

Birthdate		Ancestry	
Birth place		Social class	
Parents		Religion	
Education		Sexuality	

Significant past

Residence		Occupation	
Living with		Income	
Death?			

(attach or sketch image here)

PHYSICAL DESCRIPTION & COMMUNICATION

Body type		Language(s)	
Eyes		Voice & accent	
Hair		Literacy level	
Skin		Handwriting	
Facial express.		Eye contact	
Posture / gait		Gestures	
Grooming		Sense of humor	
Style / clothes		Show emotion?	
Accessories		Lying "tells"	
Health		Mannerisms and tics	
Noted features			

PERSONALITY

Motivators		Vulnerabilities	
Personality type		Love language	

QUESTIONNAIRE

Strengths / skills		Secrets	
Magical gifts		Fears	
Weaknesses		Hopes	
Obligations		Importants	
Accomplish.		Regrets	

What do they assume that is not true?	
What do others assume about them that's not true?	
What is their stereotype? How do they break it?	
Moral compass? When would they compromise?	
How do they react to change?	

PLOT PURPOSE

SECONDARY CHARACTER

OTHER NAMES (including titles, ranks, pseudonyms)

Age (at intro.)

Gender

Group, classification or species

Birthdate

Ancestry

Birth place

Social class

Parents

Religion

Education

Sexuality

Significant past

Residence

Occupation

Living with

Income

Death?

(attach or sketch image here)

PHYSICAL DESCRIPTION & COMMUNICATION

Body type

Language(s)

Eyes

Voice & accent

Hair

Literacy level

Skin

Handwriting

Facial express.

Eye contact

Posture / gait

Gestures

Grooming

Sense of humor

Style / clothes

Show emotion?

Accessories

Lying "tells"

Health

Mannerisms and tics

Noted features

PERSONALITY

Motivators

Vulnerabilities

Personality type

Love language

QUESTIONNAIRE

Strengths / skills

Secrets

Magical gifts

Fears

Weaknesses

Hopes

Obligations

Importants

Accomplish.

Regrets

What do they assume that is not true?

What do others assume about them that's not true?

What is their stereotype? How do they break it?

Moral compass? When would they compromise?

How do they react to change?

PLOT PURPOSE

SECONDARY CHARACTER

OTHER NAMES (including titles, ranks, pseudonyms)

Age (at intro.)

Gender

Group, classification or species

Birthdate

Birth place

Parents

Education

Ancestry

Social class

Religion

Sexuality

Significant past

Residence

Living with

Occupation

Income

Death?

(attach or sketch image here)

PHYSICAL DESCRIPTION & COMMUNICATION

Body type

Eyes

Hair

Skin

Facial express.

Posture / gait

Grooming

Style / clothes

Accessories

Health

Noted features

Language(s)

Voice & accent

Literacy level

Handwriting

Eye contact

Gestures

Sense of humor

Show emotion?

Lying "tells"

Mannerisms and tics

PERSONALITY

Motivators

Personality type

Vulnerabilities

Love language

QUESTIONNAIRE

Strengths / skills

Magical gifts

Weaknesses

Obligations

Accomplish.

Secrets

Fears

Hopes

Importants

Regrets

What do they assume that is not true?

What do others assume about them that's not true?

What is their stereotype? How do they break it?

Moral compass? When would they compromise?

How do they react to change?

PLOT PURPOSE

SECONDARY CHARACTER

OTHER NAMES
(including titles, ranks, pseudonyms)

Age (at intro.)

Gender

Group, classification or species

Birthdate

Birth place

Parents

Education

Ancestry

Social class

Religion

Sexuality

Significant past

Residence

Living with

Occupation

Income

Death?

(attach or sketch image here)

PHYSICAL DESCRIPTION & COMMUNICATION

Body type

Eyes

Hair

Skin

Facial express.

Posture / gait

Grooming

Style / clothes

Accessories

Health

Noted features

Language(s)

Voice & accent

Literacy level

Handwriting

Eye contact

Gestures

Sense of humor

Show emotion?

Lying "tells"

Mannerisms and tics

PERSONALITY

Motivators

Personality type

Vulnerabilities

Love language

QUESTIONNAIRE

Strengths / skills

Magical gifts

Weaknesses

Obligations

Accomplish.

Secrets

Fears

Hopes

Importants

Regrets

What do they assume that is not true?

What do others assume about them that's not true?

What is their stereotype? How do they break it?

Moral compass? When would they compromise?

How do they react to change?

PLOT PURPOSE

SECONDARY CHARACTER

OTHER NAMES (including titles, ranks, pseudonyms)

Age (at intro.)

Gender

Group, classification or species

Birthdate	Ancestry
Birth place	Social class
Parents	Religion
Education	Sexuality

Significant past

Residence	Occupation
Living with	Income

Death?

(attach or sketch image here)

PHYSICAL DESCRIPTION & COMMUNICATION

Body type	Language(s)
Eyes	Voice & accent
Hair	Literacy level
Skin	Handwriting
Facial express.	Eye contact
Posture / gait	Gestures
Grooming	Sense of humor
Style / clothes	Show emotion?
Accessories	Lying "tells"
Health	Mannerisms and tics
Noted features	

PERSONALITY

Motivators	Vulnerabilities
Personality type	Love language

QUESTIONNAIRE

Strengths / skills	Secrets
Magical gifts	Fears
Weaknesses	Hopes
Obligations	Importants
Accomplish.	Regrets

What do they assume that is not true?

What do others assume about them that's not true?

What is their stereotype? How do they break it?

Moral compass? When would they compromise?

How do they react to change?

PLOT PURPOSE

SECONDARY CHARACTER

OTHER NAMES (including titles, ranks, pseudonyms)

Age (at intro.)

Gender

Group, classification or species

Birthdate

Ancestry

Birth place

Social class

Parents

Religion

Education

Sexuality

Significant past

Residence

Occupation

Living with

Income

Death?

(attach or sketch image here)

PHYSICAL DESCRIPTION & COMMUNICATION

Body type

Language(s)

Eyes

Voice & accent

Hair

Literacy level

Skin

Handwriting

Facial express.

Eye contact

Posture / gait

Gestures

Grooming

Sense of humor

Style / clothes

Show emotion?

Accessories

Lying "tells"

Health

Mannerisms and tics

Noted features

PERSONALITY

Motivators

Vulnerabilities

Personality type

Love language

QUESTIONNAIRE

Strengths / skills

Secrets

Magical gifts

Fears

Weaknesses

Hopes

Obligations

Importants

Accomplish.

Regrets

What do they assume that is not true?

What do others assume about them that's not true?

What is their stereotype? How do they break it?

Moral compass? When would they compromise?

How do they react to change?

PLOT PURPOSE

SECONDARY CHARACTER

OTHER NAMES
(including titles, ranks, pseudonyms)

Age (at intro.)

Gender

Group, classification or species

Birthdate

Birth place

Parents

Education

Ancestry

Social class

Religion

Sexuality

Significant past

Residence

Living with

Occupation

Income

Death?

(attach or sketch image here)

PHYSICAL DESCRIPTION & COMMUNICATION

Body type

Eyes

Hair

Skin

Facial express.

Posture / gait

Grooming

Style / clothes

Accessories

Health

Noted features

Language(s)

Voice & accent

Literacy level

Handwriting

Eye contact

Gestures

Sense of humor

Show emotion?

Lying "tells"

Mannerisms and tics

PERSONALITY

Motivators

Personality type

Vulnerabilities

Love language

QUESTIONNAIRE

Strengths / skills

Magical gifts

Weaknesses

Obligations

Accomplish.

Secrets

Fears

Hopes

Importants

Regrets

What do they assume that is not true?

What do others assume about them that's not true?

What is their stereotype? How do they break it?

Moral compass? When would they compromise?

How do they react to change?

PLOT PURPOSE

SECONDARY CHARACTER

OTHER NAMES (including titles, ranks, pseudonyms)

Age (at intro.)

Gender

Group, classification or species

Birthdate

Birth place

Parents

Education

Ancestry

Social class

Religion

Sexuality

Significant past

Residence

Living with

Death?

Occupation

Income

(attach or sketch image here)

PHYSICAL DESCRIPTION & COMMUNICATION

Body type

Eyes

Hair

Skin

Facial express.

Posture / gait

Grooming

Style / clothes

Accessories

Health

Noted features

Language(s)

Voice & accent

Literacy level

Handwriting

Eye contact

Gestures

Sense of humor

Show emotion?

Lying "tells"

Mannerisms and tics

PERSONALITY

Motivators

Personality type

Vulnerabilities

Love language

QUESTIONNAIRE

Strengths / skills

Magical gifts

Weaknesses

Obligations

Accomplish.

Secrets

Fears

Hopes

Importants

Regrets

What do they assume that is not true?

What do others assume about them that's not true?

What is their stereotype? How do they break it?

Moral compass? When would they compromise?

How do they react to change?

PLOT PURPOSE

SECONDARY CHARACTER

OTHER NAMES (including titles, ranks, pseudonyms)

Age (at intro.)

Gender

Group, classification or species

Birthdate

Ancestry

Birth place

Social class

Parents

Religion

Education

Sexuality

Significant past

Residence

Occupation

Living with

Income

Death?

(attach or sketch image here)

PHYSICAL DESCRIPTION & COMMUNICATION

Body type

Language(s)

Eyes

Voice & accent

Hair

Literacy level

Skin

Handwriting

Facial express.

Eye contact

Posture / gait

Gestures

Grooming

Sense of humor

Style / clothes

Show emotion?

Accessories

Lying "tells"

Health

Mannerisms and tics

Noted features

PERSONALITY

Motivators

Vulnerabilities

Personality type

Love language

QUESTIONNAIRE

Strengths / skills

Secrets

Magical gifts

Fears

Weaknesses

Hopes

Obligations

Importants

Accomplish.

Regrets

What do they assume that is not true?

What do others assume about them that's not true?

What is their stereotype? How do they break it?

Moral compass? When would they compromise?

How do they react to change?

PLOT PURPOSE

SECONDARY CHARACTER

OTHER NAMES (including titles, ranks, pseudonyms)

Age (at intro.)

Gender

Group, classification or species

Birthdate

Birth place

Parents

Education

Ancestry

Social class

Religion

Sexuality

Significant past

Residence

Living with

Occupation

Income

Death?

(attach or sketch image here)

PHYSICAL DESCRIPTION & COMMUNICATION

Body type

Eyes

Hair

Skin

Facial express.

Posture / gait

Grooming

Style / clothes

Accessories

Health

Noted features

Language(s)

Voice & accent

Literacy level

Handwriting

Eye contact

Gestures

Sense of humor

Show emotion?

Lying "tells"

Mannerisms and tics

PERSONALITY

Motivators

Personality type

Vulnerabilities

Love language

QUESTIONNAIRE

Strengths / skills

Magical gifts

Weaknesses

Obligations

Accomplish.

Secrets

Fears

Hopes

Importants

Regrets

What do they assume that is not true?

What do others assume about them that's not true?

What is their stereotype? How do they break it?

Moral compass? When would they compromise?

How do they react to change?

PLOT PURPOSE

SECONDARY CHARACTER

OTHER NAMES (including titles, ranks, pseudonyms)

Age (at intro.)

Gender

Group, classification or species

Birthdate

Birth place

Parents

Education

Ancestry

Social class

Religion

Sexuality

Significant past

Residence

Living with

Occupation

Income

Death?

(attach or sketch image here)

PHYSICAL DESCRIPTION & COMMUNICATION

Body type

Eyes

Hair

Skin

Facial express.

Posture / gait

Grooming

Style / clothes

Accessories

Health

Noted features

Language(s)

Voice & accent

Literacy level

Handwriting

Eye contact

Gestures

Sense of humor

Show emotion?

Lying "tells"

Mannerisms and tics

PERSONALITY

Motivators

Personality type

Vulnerabilities

Love language

QUESTIONNAIRE

Strengths / skills

Magical gifts

Weaknesses

Obligations

Accomplish.

Secrets

Fears

Hopes

Importants

Regrets

What do they assume that is not true?

What do others assume about them that's not true?

What is their stereotype? How do they break it?

Moral compass? When would they compromise?

How do they react to change?

PLOT PURPOSE

SECONDARY CHARACTER

OTHER NAMES (including titles, ranks, pseudonyms)

Age (at intro.)

Gender

Group, classification or species

Birthdate

Birth place

Parents

Education

Ancestry

Social class

Religion

Sexuality

Significant past

Residence

Living with

Occupation

Income

Death?

(attach or sketch image here)

PHYSICAL DESCRIPTION & COMMUNICATION

Body type

Eyes

Hair

Skin

Facial express.

Posture / gait

Grooming

Style / clothes

Accessories

Health

Noted features

Language(s)

Voice & accent

Literacy level

Handwriting

Eye contact

Gestures

Sense of humor

Show emotion?

Lying "tells"

Mannerisms and tics

PERSONALITY

Motivators

Personality type

Vulnerabilities

Love language

QUESTIONNAIRE

Strengths / skills

Magical gifts

Weaknesses

Obligations

Accomplish.

Secrets

Fears

Hopes

Importants

Regrets

What do they assume that is not true?

What do others assume about them that's not true?

What is their stereotype? How do they break it?

Moral compass? When would they compromise?

How do they react to change?

PLOT PURPOSE

MINOR
CHARACTERS

"An author should know their character intimately, they should know their history, how they would react in a situation, they should know their look and mannerisms down to the smallest facial tick. Yet all of this need not be revealed to the reader."

— Aaron Miles, *On Character Construction*

Name

Appearance

Good to know

Name

Appearance

Good to know

Name

Appearance

Good to know

Name

Appearance

Good to know

Name

Appearance

Good to know

Name

Appearance

Good to know

Name

Appearance

Good to know

Name

Appearance

Good to know

Name

Appearance

Good to know

Name

Appearance

Good to know

Name

Appearance

Good to know

Name

Appearance

Good to know

Name

Appearance

Good to know

Name

Appearance

Good to know

Name

Appearance

Good to know

Name

Appearance

Good to know

Name

Appearance

Good to know

Name

Appearance

Good to know

Name

Appearance

Good to know

Name

Appearance

Good to know

Name

Appearance

Good to know

Name

Appearance

Good to know

Name

Appearance

Good to know

Name

Appearance

Good to know

Name

Appearance

Good to know

Name

Appearance

Good to know

Name

Appearance

Good to know

Name

Appearance

Good to know

Name

Appearance

Good to know

Name

Appearance

Good to know

Name

Appearance

Good to know

Name

Appearance

Good to know

Name

Appearance

Good to know

Name

Appearance

Good to know

Name

Appearance

Good to know

Name

Appearance

Good to know

Name

Appearance

Good to know

Name

Appearance

Good to know

Name

Appearance

Good to know

Name

Appearance

Good to know

Name

Appearance

Good to know

Name

Appearance

Good to know

Name

Appearance

Good to know

Name

Appearance

Good to know

Name

Appearance

Good to know

Name

Appearance

Good to know

Name

Appearance

Good to know

Name

Appearance

Good to know

Name

Appearance

Good to know

Name

Appearance

Good to know

Name

Appearance

Good to know

Name

Appearance

Good to know

Name

Appearance

Good to know

Name

Appearance

Good to know

Name

Appearance

Good to know

Name

Appearance

Good to know

Name

Appearance

Good to know

Name

Appearance

Good to know

Name

Appearance

Good to know

Name

Appearance

Good to know

Name

Appearance

Good to know

Name

Appearance

Good to know

Name

Appearance

Good to know

Name

Appearance

Good to know

Name

Appearance

Good to know

Name

Appearance

Good to know

Name

Appearance

Good to know

Name

Appearance

Good to know

Name

Appearance

Good to know

Name

Appearance

Good to know

Name

Appearance

Good to know

Name

Appearance

Good to know

Name

Appearance

Good to know

Name

Appearance

Good to know

Name

Appearance

Good to know

Name

Appearance

Good to know

Name

Appearance

Good to know

Name

Appearance

Good to know

Name

Appearance

Good to know

Name

Appearance

Good to know

Name

Appearance

Good to know

Name

Appearance

Good to know

Name

Appearance

Good to know

Name

Appearance

Good to know

Name

Appearance

Good to know

Name

Appearance

Good to know

Name

Appearance

Good to know

Name

Appearance

Good to know

Name

Appearance

Good to know

Name

Appearance

Good to know

Name

Appearance

Good to know

Name

Appearance

Good to know

Name

Appearance

Good to know

Name

Appearance

Good to know

Name

Appearance

Good to know

Name

Appearance

Good to know

Name

Appearance

Good to know

Name

Appearance

Good to know

Name

Appearance

Good to know

Name

Appearance

Good to know

Name

Appearance

Good to know

Name

Appearance

Good to know

Name

Appearance

Good to know

Name

Appearance

Good to know

Name

Appearance

Good to know

Name

Appearance

Good to know

Name

Appearance

Good to know

Name

Appearance

Good to know

GROUPS

"The best way to know your character's point of view is to know their background. You should understand why do they see the world a certain way. You should know how they perceive things the way they do."

— Skylar Spring, *Creating Lifelike Characters: It's All In The Details*

GROUP

Innate purpose

Location

Time frame

Requirements

GOOD GUYS

BAD GUYS

NEUTRAL

Plot purpose or story arc

History

LIST

	NAME	LABEL	DESCRIPTION
1			
2			
3			
4			
5			
6			
7			
8			
9			
10			
11			
12			
13			
14			
15			
16			
17			
18			
19			
20			
21			
22			
23			
24			
25			
26			
27			
28			
29			
30			

OTHER INFO

Innate purpose		GOOD GUYS
Location		BAD GUYS
Time frame		NEUTRAL
Requirements		

Plot purpose or story arc

History

LIST

	NAME	LABEL	DESCRIPTION
1			
2			
3			
4			
5			
6			
7			
8			
9			
10			
11			
12			
13			
14			
15			
16			
17			
18			
19			
20			
21			
22			
23			
24			
25			
26			
27			
28			
29			
30			

OTHER INFO

GROUP

Innate purpose	
Location	
Time frame	
Requirements	

GOOD GUYS

BAD GUYS

NEUTRAL

Plot purpose or story arc

History

LIST

	NAME	LABEL	DESCRIPTION
1			
2			
3			
4			
5			
6			
7			
8			
9			
10			
11			
12			
13			
14			
15			
16			
17			
18			
19			
20			
21			
22			
23			
24			
25			
26			
27			
28			
29			
30			

OTHER INFO

Innate purpose	
Location	
Time frame	
Requirements	

GOOD GUYS

BAD GUYS

NEUTRAL

Plot purpose or story arc

History

LIST

	NAME	LABEL	DESCRIPTION
1			
2			
3			
4			
5			
6			
7			
8			
9			
10			
11			
12			
13			
14			
15			
16			
17			
18			
19			
20			
21			
22			
23			
24			
25			
26			
27			
28			
29			
30			

OTHER INFO

GROUP

Innate purpose

Location

Time frame

Requirements

GOOD GUYS	
BAD GUYS	
NEUTRAL	

Plot purpose or story arc

History

LIST

	NAME	LABEL	DESCRIPTION
1			
2			
3			
4			
5			
6			
7			
8			
9			
10			
11			
12			
13			
14			
15			
16			
17			
18			
19			
20			
21			
22			
23			
24			
25			
26			
27			
28			
29			
30			

OTHER INFO

Innate purpose	
Location	
Time frame	
Requirements	

GOOD GUYS
BAD GUYS
NEUTRAL

Plot purpose or story arc

History

LIST

	NAME	LABEL	DESCRIPTION
1			
2			
3			
4			
5			
6			
7			
8			
9			
10			
11			
12			
13			
14			
15			
16			
17			
18			
19			
20			
21			
22			
23			
24			
25			
26			
27			
28			
29			
30			

OTHER INFO

GROUP

Innate purpose

Location

Time frame

Requirements

	GOOD GUYS
	BAD GUYS
	NEUTRAL

Plot
purpose or
story arc

History

LIST

	NAME	LABEL	DESCRIPTION
1			
2			
3			
4			
5			
6			
7			
8			
9			
10			
11			
12			
13			
14			
15			
16			
17			
18			
19			
20			
21			
22			
23			
24			
25			
26			
27			
28			
29			
30			

OTHER INFO

Innate purpose

Location

Time frame

Requirements

GOOD GUYS		
BAD GUYS		
NEUTRAL		

Plot purpose or story arc

History

LIST

	NAME	LABEL	DESCRIPTION
1			
2			
3			
4			
5			
6			
7			
8			
9			
10			
11			
12			
13			
14			
15			
16			
17			
18			
19			
20			
21			
22			
23			
24			
25			
26			
27			
28			
29			
30			

OTHER INFO

GROUP

Innate purpose

Location

Time frame

Requirements

| GOOD GUYS |
| BAD GUYS |
| NEUTRAL |

Plot purpose or story arc

History

LIST

	NAME	LABEL	DESCRIPTION
1			
2			
3			
4			
5			
6			
7			
8			
9			
10			
11			
12			
13			
14			
15			
16			
17			
18			
19			
20			
21			
22			
23			
24			
25			
26			
27			
28			
29			
30			

OTHER INFO

Innate purpose	
Location	
Time frame	
Requirements	

GOOD GUYS

BAD GUYS

NEUTRAL

Plot purpose or story arc

History

LIST

	NAME	LABEL	DESCRIPTION
1			
2			
3			
4			
5			
6			
7			
8			
9			
10			
11			
12			
13			
14			
15			
16			
17			
18			
19			
20			
21			
22			
23			
24			
25			
26			
27			
28			
29			
30			

OTHER INFO

GROUP

Innate purpose	
Location	
Time frame	
Requirements	

GOOD GUYS

BAD GUYS

NEUTRAL

Plot purpose or story arc

History

LIST

	NAME	LABEL	DESCRIPTION
1			
2			
3			
4			
5			
6			
7			
8			
9			
10			
11			
12			
13			
14			
15			
16			
17			
18			
19			
20			
21			
22			
23			
24			
25			
26			
27			
28			
29			
30			

OTHER INFO

Innate purpose

Location

Time frame

Requirements

	GOOD GUYS
	BAD GUYS
	NEUTRAL

Plot purpose or story arc

History

LIST

	NAME	LABEL	DESCRIPTION
1			
2			
3			
4			
5			
6			
7			
8			
9			
10			
11			
12			
13			
14			
15			
16			
17			
18			
19			
20			
21			
22			
23			
24			
25			
26			
27			
28			
29			
30			

OTHER INFO

GROUP

Innate purpose	
Location	
Time frame	
Requirements	

GOOD GUYS

BAD GUYS

NEUTRAL

Plot purpose or story arc

History

LIST

	NAME	LABEL	DESCRIPTION
1			
2			
3			
4			
5			
6			
7			
8			
9			
10			
11			
12			
13			
14			
15			
16			
17			
18			
19			
20			
21			
22			
23			
24			
25			
26			
27			
28			
29			
30			

OTHER INFO

MAPS & TREES

"I trace all relationships that character might have throughout the plot. I then list emotions that the character will experience in the relationships with those other characters. I often refer back to this list when writing dialogue to ensure that the feelings expressed are genuine and real."

— Roger Colby, *Character Development: A Step by Step Method*

When character mapping, show good, bad, and complicated relationships. A variety of interconnected relationships culminating in complicated relational triangles can lead to fantastic story conflict and tension.

(Example character map)

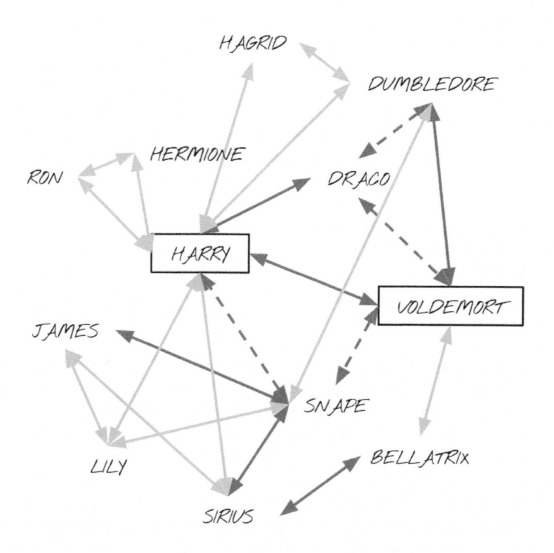

NOTES

"Developing a character with genuine depth requires a focus on not just desire but how the character deals with frustration of her desires, as well as her vulnerabilities, her secrets, and especially her contradictions. This development needs to be forged in scenes, the better to employ your intuition rather than your intellect."

— David Corbett, *The Art of Character: Creating Memorable Characters for Fiction, Film, and TV*

LISTS

"Redeemability involves more than just actions. We've seen lots and lots of characters in novels and movies who do utterly horrible things and yet we love them anyway. But if characters are going to consistently do bad things and retain the reader's sympathy: they have to be likable. They have to be brave or brilliant or hilarious or charismatic or strong or all of the above."

— Nathan Bransford, *Sympathetic vs. Unsympathetic Characters*

Consider using pencil, or spacing out additions as you go. This list could be very fluid until you have a final draft.

A

B

C

D

E

F

G

A

H

I

J

K

L

M

N

O

P

Q

R

S

T

U

V

W

X

Y

Z

OTHER

Made in the USA
Las Vegas, NV
04 September 2024

94797279R00090